NEXT LEVEL PREP:

A College and Career Readiness Journal

TENEKA ADAMS

JayMedia
Publishing

ISBN: 978-1-957443-08-9
First printing, 2023.

JayMedia Publishing
Laurel, MD 20708

ACKNOWLEDGEMENTS

For Jasmin, Cleavon, Jr., Jessica, and Xavier. You are my inspiration, as I have spent much time with you all, following a lot of these steps. Your steps are ordered by God before the foundation of the world.

Level Up at Ridgley Ministries Church of God in Christ, I'd like to thank you for pulling this journal out of me. It's been in me for some years now, since my grown daughter was in Middle School.

Delia, I so appreciate all your input and finishing touches. Thank you for your contributions to this publication. You are such a blessing and I'm glad that you are on my team!

Mom, thank you for ALWAYS encouraging me and making sure that I have what I need to keep moving forward.

Wonderful husband of mine, thank you so much for titling this publication when I was not sure what to call it. Let's take it to the Next Level!!

INTRODUCTION

Overwhelming, stressful, confusing, and scary are some of the words that come to mind when students are trying to prepare for life after high school. However, the word exciting can also be used to describe this time. The great news is that this journal is designed to help students keep their information in order and one place and to help them transition from high school to the paths they may choose to take afterward.

This journal is not meant for students to do in isolation but should be used to guide conversations that parents, guardians, mentors, and teachers can have to help the student gather ideas and plan their next steps.

TABLE OF CONTENTS

1

GETTING TO KNOW YOU

This portion of your journal begins by taking you, the student, through the process of homing in on things that you are interested in, things that you are good at, things you know, and things that bring you joy. We begin the journal this way because sometimes it can be challenging as a youth or young adult to imagine where you will be in the future or what type of career path you will travel as an adult. Doing what you love and finding something you are passionate about could be beneficial. We understand these things can change, but we will start here.

WHAT ARE SOME THINGS THAT YOU ARE INTERESTED IN?

1. _____

2. _____

3. _____

4. _____

5. _____

WHAT ARE SOME THINGS THAT YOU ARE GOOD AT?

1. _____

2. _____

3. _____

4. _____

5. _____

WHAT DO YOU HAVE A LOT OF KNOWLEDGE ABOUT?

1. _____

2. _____

3. _____

4. _____

5. _____

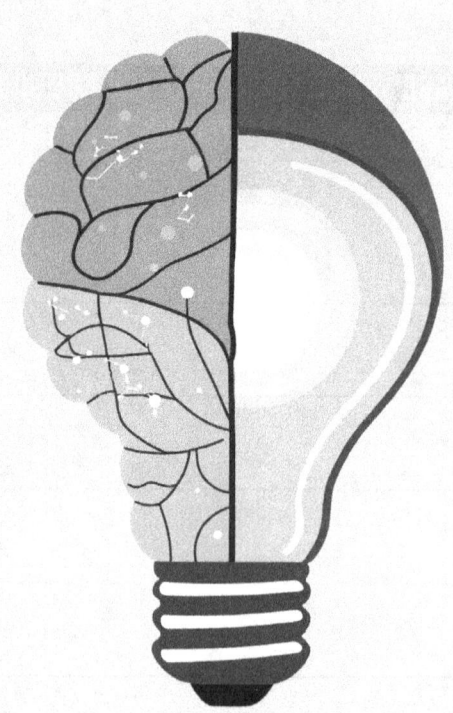

WHAT ARE SOME THINGS YOU DO THAT BRING YOU JOY?

1. _____

2. _____

3. _____

4. _____

5. _____

"Whatever you do, work at it with all your heart, as working for the Lord, not for human masters"

— Colossians 3:23 (NIV)

EXTRACURRICULAR ACTIVITIES & HIGH SCHOOL PROGRAMS

In this section, explore the extracurricular activities you have participated in, are currently participating in, and would like to participate in. Take notice of how you performed while participating in these activities and programs. Evaluate whether you are flourishing or whether you are struggling. It is also important to acknowledge that some activities and programs people get involved in are simply because a parent wanted them to or because a friend is doing that particular activity. Therefore, in this section, please focus on the programs and activities you did well in and those you would like to participate in and make a point to sign up for those in the future.

BELOW ARE SOME EXAMPLES:

Art:
Art Club, Drama Club, Fashion Design, Graphic Design, Photography

Community:
4-H, Habitat for Humanity, Key Club

Leadership:
Beta Club, Peer Leadership

Government:
Student Council, Student Government

Media:
Newspaper, Radio station, Yearbook Committee

Military:
Junior ROTC

Music:
School Chorus, Ensembles, Marching Band

Performance Art:
Dance, Poetry Club

Special Interest:
Boy Scouts, Chess Club, Future Business Leaders of America (FBLA), Girl Scouts

Speech and Political Interest:
Debate Club, Mock Trial, Toastmasters

Sports and Recreation:
Baseball/Softball, Basketball, Cheerleading, Football, Golf, Wrestling, Swimming, Tennis, Volleyball, Soccer, Track & Field

Volunteer:
Church Outreach, Mentoring, Tutoring, Local Charities, Local Soup Kitchen

PLEASE LIST ACTIVITIES AND PROGRAMS YOU HAVE BEEN INVOLVED IN, DID WELL IN, OR EXCELLED IN.

1. _____

2. _____

3. _____

4. _____

5. _____

6. _____

7. _____

8. _____

9. _____

10. _____

WHAT ACTIVITIES OR PROGRAMS *WOULD YOU LIKE* TO BE INVOLVED IN?

1. _____

2. _____

3. _____

4. _____

5. _____

"Commit your work to the Lord, and your plans will succeed."

— PROVERBS 16:3 (CEB)

INTEREST AND EXPERTISE ALIGNED PROGRAMS

Serious business starts here as you identify the patterns that let you know what career paths you might be interested in. Revisit your lists to determine what extra-curricular activities you would like to participate in when you go to high school. Think about what sports you might want to play in high school. Think of what programs you would like to participate in in high school. (These do not necessarily have to be classes but could be things you would stay after school for).

I WANT TO ATTEND A HIGH SCHOOL THAT HAS THE FOLLOWING PROGRAMS AND EXTRACURRICULAR ACTIVITIES:

1. _____

2. _____

3. _____

4. _____

5. _____

Now, it is time to research **local high schools with programs you are interested in being a part of**. Having a parent or guardian do this with you may be a good idea. Once you have compiled this list, visit their website and see if there are exams that need to be taken before students can participate in specific programs that you may want to be involved in. Also, look at application deadlines to put them on your calendar.

1. _____

2. _____

3. _____

4. _____

5. _____

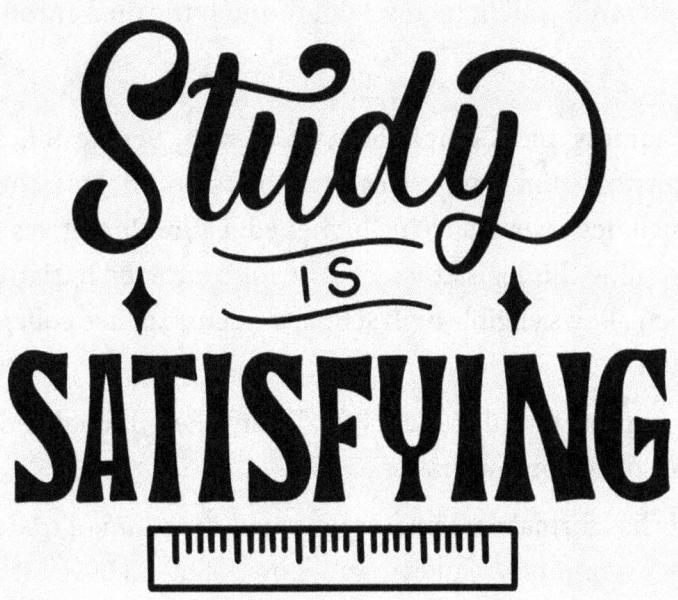

What is dual enrollment?

Dual enrollment is a program that allows high school students to take college courses and earn college credit before they graduate. Students are enrolled in high school and college at the same time.

What is the difference between dual enrollment and dual credit?

Simply put, students who participate in dual enrollment programs take college courses and only earn college credit. Students in dual credit programs take college courses and simultaneously earn high school and college credits.

What are the benefits of dual enrollment?

There are several reasons to consider obtaining college credit while still in high school. Dual enrollment programs help you to save time and money, allow you to take classes that your high school does not offer, understand the expectations of college-level courses earlier, and explore your interests before choosing a major.

Website: https://www.act.org/content/act/en/students-and-parents/high-school-success/high-school-resources/dual-enrollment-faqs.html

About the Program

In keeping with Prince George's County Public School's (PGCPS) goal to ensure that every child is college and career-ready, PGCPS high school juniors and seniors could earn college credit while still in high school through the dual enrollment program.

Background

The College Readiness and Completion Act of 2013, Senate Bill 740, establishes several requirements to increase college readiness and degree completion in the State. The bill includes several specific higher education initiatives from across the nation that streamline this legislative act. The Bill's targeted initiatives include dual enrollment, which allows eligible high school students to take college courses while still in high school.

PGCPS will pay tuition for all students dually enrolled in qualified courses at any Maryland public college or university.

PGCPS currently has formal agreements and memorandum of understanding with Prince George's Community College and Bowie State University. Students can receive dual credit (credit appearing on a student's college and high school transcript) as a benefit of the deal—additionally, the college shares student grades directly with PGCPS. If students participate in Dual Enrollment at an institution where PGCPS does not have a formal agreement, grades must be submitted to the student's high school to be added to their high school transcript.

Website: https://www.pgcps.org/offices/dual-enrollment

Note that if you live in a different state or county, you must research to find the information for those specific offices in your area.

"Even youths grow tired and weary, and young men stumble and fall; but those who hope in the LORD will renew their strength. They will soar on wings like eagles; they will run and not grow weary, they will walk and not be faint."

– ISAIAH 40:30-31 (NIV)

4

ACADEMIC ACHIEVEMENTS, AWARDS, AND RECOGNITIONS

Here is where you will track all your academic achievements, extra-curricular awards, recognitions, etc. You will be able to use these on your college applications, as well as your resume. A coach, employer, club adviser, teacher, counselor, principal, or pastor are all examples of people you may ask for a recommendation letter from. (Note: anyone that can say a lot about your skills and character)

1. _____

2. _____

3. _____

4. _____

5. _____

GRADES & CLASSES

- Make education a priority

GET INVOLVED

- Sports
- Clubs
- Volunteer

ACT/SAT

- FREE online practice exams to practice for standardized tests.

COLLEGE SEARCH

- Research potential schools
- Schedule campus visits

REQUEST LETTERS OF RECOMMENDATION

College Applications

- Write a personal essay
- Complete college applications

Financial Aid

- Complete The FAFSA
- Request FSA ID
- Apply for scholarships

Make Your Decision

- Choose schools as early as you can
- Send final high school transcript

Note that early commitment before the primary deadline may lead to additional scholarship opportunities from the school you choose to attend.

5

COLLEGES, UNIVERSITIES, OR TECHNICAL SCHOOLS

COLLEGES, UNIVERSITIES, AND TECHNICAL SCHOOLS YOU HAVE APPLIED TO:

1. _____

2. _____

3. _____

4. _____

5. _____

6. _____

7. _____

8. _____

9. _____

COLLEGE TOURS THAT YOU WOULD LIKE TO GO ON AND DETAILS OF THOSE TOURS.

_____

_____

_____

_____

_____

_____

_____

_____

_____

WE CHALLENGE YOU TO RESEARCH CAREERS THAT MATCH YOUR INTERESTS AND AREAS OF EXPERTISE!

1. _____

2. _____

3. _____

4. _____

5. _____

"I have been young, and now am old, yet I have not seen the righteous forsaken or his children begging for bread."

- Psalm 37:25 (ESV)

6

SCHOLARSHIPS

Scholarships are grants or payments made to support a student's education, awarded based on academic or other achievement. This is money that does not have to be paid back.

You will have to keep track of the scholarships you apply for, the scholarships you receive, and the various usernames and passwords that go to those websites and accounts. There are merit-based scholarships and need-based scholarships that students may apply for. The merit-based scholarships usually involve higher test scores or higher grade point averages. Need-based scholarships could include those that look at parents or household income, single-parent homes, hardships, etc. But do not worry; we have included a few websites with all kinds of scholarships and databases with the requirements and deadlines listed. Students can check them every year.

https://www.scholarships.com/

https://www.fastweb.com/

https://www.cbcfinc.org/programs/scholarships/

https://finaid.org/scholarships/

https://mhec.maryland.gov/preparing/Pages/FinancialAid/descriptions.aspx

SCHOLARSHIPS APPLIED TO:	WEBSITE USERNAME & PASSWORD	RECEIVED (Y/N)

"Keep this Book of the Law always on your lips; meditate on it day and night, so that you may be careful to do everything written in it. Then you will be prosperous and successful."

- JOSHUA 1:8 (NIV)

LIVING ARRANGEMENTS

In this section, you will consider where you may live after high school. The answer is different for everyone when they graduate. Some people go live on campus where they will be attending college. Others may decide not to go to college, immediately enter the workforce, and get an apartment alone if the salary can sustain this expense. Some also get roommates, rent an apartment or townhouse, and split the rent to be more manageable than paying the entire amount alone. Yet others choose to stay at home with a parent or guardian until financial stability is established. Below are some questions to consider.

WHERE CAN YOU AFFORD TO LIVE?

LOCATION OR NAME OF NEIGHBORHOOD	RENT/MORTGAGE

While considering where you will live, consider how you will get where you need to go. Will you use public transportation? Do you or will you have your vehicle? Will you live and work in an area where you can walk to work?

Please note that when living alone, there will be other expenses like utilities, groceries, gas, entertainment, etc. These are all things to think about in addition to the rent. Your salary (how much money you make in a year for a particular job) should be able to sustain all your living expenses. And if you do not make enough money per year to afford to live on your own or have your own transportation, adjustments may need to be made regarding your career choices.

USE THIS SPACE TO MAKE NOTES ABOUT THINGS MENTIONED PREVIOUSLY

CONCLUSION

The goal of this college and career readiness journal is to be used as a guide. It certainly gives students a lot to think about. Throughout these pages, hopefully, you were able to take productive steps that can and will lead you through life after high school. Feel free to revisit as much as necessary.

www.ingramcontent.com/pod-product-compliance
Lightning Source LLC
Chambersburg PA
CBHW081006140626
46546CB00019B/3457